THE OFFICIAL

RANGERS
ANNUAL 2011

Written by Douglas Russell

A Grange Publication

© 2010. Published by Grange Communications Ltd., Edinburgh, under licence from Rangers Football Club. Printed in the EU.

Photographs © Rangers Football Club & Press Association Images

ISBN 978-1-907104-72-5

£7.99

CONTENTS

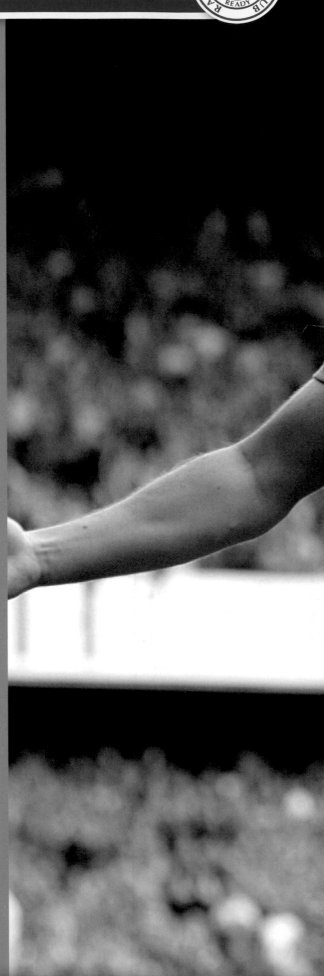

Champions Again!

AUGUST

The cheers and applause that greeted the unfurling of the Club's 52nd league championship flag had barely drifted away when Lee McCulloch opened the scoring against Falkirk with the day's quickest SPL goal. The fans' reaction to this magnificent strike — a thunderous drive from 30 yards that screamed into the top corner — virtually raised the stadium roof for a second time that afternoon. Although Finnigan equalised for the visitors, Kenny Miller headed home from a Steven Davis chipped cross to make it 2-1 before half time. The Scotland striker extended Rangers lead in the second period after a searing run from deep ended with a clinical left foot finish past Olejnik. Then, near the end, Miller set up Steven Naismith who outpaced McNamara to net his side's fourth of the afternoon. This win was the Club's 10th straight victory over Falkirk in all competitions.

Rangers came from a goal behind — and a man down — to clinch victory in memorable fashion at the end of a dramatic encounter at Tynecastle.

Following Kevin Thomson's early dismissal for a late challenge, Hearts striker David Witteveen hit the only goal of a pulsating first half. Walter Smith's men, despite their numerical disadvantage, dominated the second period however and it came as little surprise when Rangers drew level. Lee McCulloch claimed the equaliser with a powerful penalty box header following Steven Smith's free kick. Then, right at the death, substitute Kris Boyd clinched victory with an emphatic finish from the penalty spot after Steven Naismith was bundled over going for goal.

Doubles from both Kris Boyd and Steven Whittaker ensured a comfortable win over Hamilton Academical at Ibrox. Following Steven Davis' precise pass, full back Whittaker opened the scoring early in the first half with a fierce drive across Cerny from the edge of the area. Boyd, unchallenged, headed home to double Rangers tally before the break. The striker's second of the

afternoon ended a flowing move when he swept home an emphatic left foot finish after Steven Naismith's cutback. The pick of the goals, however, belonged to Whittaker. His wonderful low strike from twenty yards (that curled just beyond the keeper at the far post) was worth the price of admission alone. On a day when several individual displays caught the eye, Steven Davis topped the poll with a richly deserved man of the match award.

SEPTEMBER

Although Madjid Bougherra came close with a header just before the break, opportunities for Rangers were few and far between in the first half against Motherwell at Fir Park. The arrival of substitutes Steven Naismith and Nacho Novo (fifteen minutes into the second period) changed the tempo of play but a breakthrough goal still failed to arrive. Right at the end, Allan McGregor's brilliant block from an O'Brien penalty denied the Lanarkshire men a late winner.

Away to Kilmarnock, Walter Smith's side dropped points for the second Saturday lunchtime in succession following another no-score draw. Despite the fact that nine yellow and two red cards were brandished (Pedro Mendes and Kilmarnock's Manuel Pascali were dismissed in the first and second half respectively), the game was certainly not a bad tempered affair. Allan McGregor was again in exceptional form making fine saves from both Hamill and Sammon.

Despite an abundance of pressure – particularly in the first forty five minutes – the Light Blues failed to find the back of the net for the third SPL fixture in a row. Certainly visitors Aberdeen defended well to survive an early onslaught and grew in confidence as the game progressed but this was a fixture that Rangers really should have won considering their overall dominance.

OCTOBER

Two early first half goals from Kenny Miller ensured victory in the opening Old Firm clash of the campaign. His first of the game was a right foot finish past Celtic keeper Boruc following Kris Boyd's defence-splitting pass. Then, capitalising on Allan McGregor's long kick out, the Scotland striker out-muscled central defender Loovens to the bouncing ball before shooting beyond Boruc for number two. Although McGeady scored from the penalty spot ten minutes later, the Celtic revival would go no further and Rangers held firm for the rest of the game to secure three crucial points. This was Walter Smith's 25th Old Firm win as a Manager.

Managed by former Rangers player Derek McInnes, SPL newcomers St Johnstone took a deserved lead through Samuels before Kris Boyd (with a deadly swing of his right foot) squared it from eight yards just before the break. Full back Sasa Papac was the unlikely match winner when, towards the end of the ninety minutes, his superb left foot drive from the edge of the area beat veteran keeper Main to ensure full points in Perth. With Celtic drawing at home to Motherwell, Rangers returned to the top of the SPL table.

Against Hibernian at Ibrox, a thrilling game of football ended all-square at 1-1. Rangers opened the scoring after eight minutes when Kris Boyd (with his fifth league goal of the 2009/10 campaign) volleyed home following Kyle Lafferty's inviting header. Both keepers then produced several fine saves before Stokes, deep into the second period, equalised for the Edinburgh side with a fine individual effort that won the Clydesdale Bank 2009/10 Goal of the Season award.

NOVEMBER

Kris Boyd's SPL goal tally rose to seven after he claimed a brace in the 2-1 home win over St Mirren. In the first minute, keeper Gallacher could only parry John Fleck's thumping shot towards the far post and Boyd was on hand to score from close range. The striker hit his second of the afternoon shortly after the break when he converted Nacho Novo's drive across the face of the goal. Although O'Donnell claimed a consolation just before the final whistle, Boyd's contribution was the crucial factor.

Continuing a rich vein of form, Kris Boyd hit his side's opening goal for the fourth league game in a row. This early strike against Kilmarnock (from Kevin Thomson's superb through-ball) was followed by another two first half goals. Kenny Miller netted the first of these after good play by Lee McCulloch. Scorer then turned provider when Miller set up Steven Whittaker who drilled home with his left foot after his initial effort was blocked. Allan McGregor was mightily impressive once again with a string of important stops.

Walter Smith's side, unbeaten in the SPL since March, came unstuck at Pittodrie when Lee Miller's first half goal was enough to secure all three points for Aberdeen. Despite enjoying the bulk of possession for most of the game and creating some real chances, Rangers could not force an equaliser.

DECEMBER

The Light Blues really clicked into gear in December, however, and their form would provide the platform for another SPL title. It all began at Falkrik's Westfield Stadium when two clinical finishes from Kris Boyd set Rangers on the road to a convincing 3-1 win. Although the hosts pulled one back just before the break, Kenny Miller's blasted penalty in the second half put distance between the sides. Boyd, with 151 league goals in total, was now only seven short of former Celt Henrik Larsson's SPL scoring record. Incidentally, this was David Weir's 100th SPL appearance for Rangers and it coincided with a game against one of his former clubs.

The following week, Kris Boyd again made his mark early-on and, for the second time in just five league games, the striker netted in the first minute. His opener against St Johnstone at Ibrox – a sweet left foot strike from just outside the area – was supplemented with a converted penalty after Nacho Novo had been brought down by Graeme Smith, the former Rangers keeper. Novo himself made it 3-0 at the start of the second period when the livewire Spaniard drilled home after a Kenny Miller shot had been blocked.

The rearranged fixture with Dundee United at Tannadice – the November game had been abandoned at half time due to a waterlogged pitch – was one of the best displays of the season by Rangers. DaMarcus Beasley, with his first goal since the 2008 Scottish Cup final, opened the scoring in the first half when his stunning left foot shot from the angle of the box swerved and dipped before finding the far corner of the net. After the break, Kenny Miller netted twice. His first of the evening was a powerful downward header after Nacho Novo had waltzed away from three challenges before delivering a perfect cross into the area. Then, collecting a Beasley pass, the Scotland striker twisted past Dixon and fired home from close range to complete his double and a very impressive 3-0 win for the defending League Champions.

Against Motherwell at Ibrox, the home fans were treated to an early Christmas present as stylish Rangers cruised to a 6-1 win. Kenny Miller opened the scoring shortly after kick-off with a sublime

right foot strike from 22 yards that sailed over keeper Ruddy and into the net off the underside of the crossbar. Into the second period, Kris Boyd made it 2-0 (following an inch-perfect Davis pass into the box) before Miller claimed his second of the afternoon, slipping home from a tight angle. After Hutchinson pulled one back for the visitors, substitute Kyle Lafferty (2) and on-form winger DaMarcus Beasley completed the rout. Rangers had now scored in the first ten minutes of each of their last five home games and struck 15 goals in four league fixtures.

Despite falling behind to a Hibernian goal in the very first minute at Easter Road, Rangers responded like champions and by half time were ahead in the capital clash thanks to goals from Kenny Miller (driving home from a clever Kris Boyd pass) and Boyd himself with an emphatic close range finish. Then, after the break, Nacho Novo beat Ma-Kalambay at the near post before Miller completed his double to confirm a comprehensive 4-1 result in Edinburgh. Between them, Boyd and Miller had now scored 26 goals this season.

Walter Smith's side, on a remarkable night in Govan, ended the year on the highest of highs with an astonishing 7-1 win over Dundee United. Following a first half hat-trick by Kris Boyd (a trio

of penalty, right foot finish and left foot finish that was bagged inside nine minutes), the visitors pulled one back at the start of the second period before substitute Steven Whittaker, Boyd (2) and Madjid Bougherra – with a magnificent solo effort – added another four to complete the demolition of the team from the City of Discovery. There was even further cause for celebration as 2009 came to a close – Kris Boyd, with 160 career goals, was now top of the all-time SPL scoring charts, having overtaken Henrik Larsson's previous record of 158.

JANUARY

Celtic, dominating the second Old Firm meeting of the league season, had victory in sight when substitute Scott McDonald scored late in the second half. Two minutes later, however, Lee McCulloch rescued a point for Rangers when his bullet header (following a Steven Davis corner) silenced the home support. Right at the end, Allan McGregor produced a truly world class save to deny Greek striker Samaras whose shot seemed to have 'goal' written all over it.

One week after drawing 3-3 with Hamilton Academical in the Active Nation Scottish Cup, the Light Blues returned to New Douglas Park on league duty. Nacho Novo partnered Kyle Lafferty in attack as both Kris Boyd (injured) and Kenny Miller (suspended) missed the game. Although the home side created the better of the chances throughout the ninety minutes, Novo sealed victory by scoring the only goal of the game when he slotted home from a tight angle after keeper Cerny parried a left foot drive from second half substitute John Fleck.

Fleck, on from the start, joined Kyle Lafferty upfront for the visit of Hearts on a day when injury prevented strikers Boyd, Miller and Novo from participating. Although the Tynecastle outfit – unbeaten in their previous six league outings – took the lead late in the second half, substitute Andrew Little secured a point in stoppage time when he guided home from close range after the keeper failed to hold a powerful Lee McCulloch shot from the edge of the area. It was the young Ulsterman's first senior goal for the Club.

At New St Mirren Park, inside the opening
two minutes, Steven Davis beat the offside
trap to score his first goal of the season
and give Rangers the best possible start in Paisley.
Then, right at the end of the game, Nacho Novo
made it 2-0 after cutting in from the right before
clipping home off the inside of the far post. Celtic's
defeat at home to Hibernian meant that Walter
Smith's side, albeit having played one more game
than their city rivals, now enjoyed a ten point
advantage at the top of the league table.

Three days later, against Falkirk at Ibrox, Steven
Davis again opened the scoring when his sublime
free-kick from the edge of the area beat Olejnik
at the keeper's right hand side. In the second half,
John Fleck (taking advantage of an inch perfect
Davis pass to net at the far post) and Steven
Whittaker (striding into the box to thump home for
his ninth goal of the season) were both acclaimed
as the Light Blues recorded a 3-0 win.

13

FEBRUARY

In-form Motherwell (four wins in their previous five league games and yet to concede a goal in 2010) took a well deserved first half lead at Fir Park when Tom Hateley's stunning free-kick beat Allan McGregor. After the break, however, Rangers fought back bravely to earn a vital SPL point. Kris Boyd was the hero once again and scored his 20th goal of the season when he tapped home from close range following Sasa Papac's cross. Celtic's win over Hearts meant that Rangers lead at the top of the SPL was now eight points with the same number of games played.

Following a draw and a win at Ibrox and Celtic Park respectively, Hibernian had yet to lose in Glasgow this season. On Valentine's Day, however, hosts Rangers proved too strong and emerged from an engrossing Sunday lunchtime encounter with a crucial 3-0 victory. After an evenly matched first half, Steven Whittaker opened the scoring against his former club in the second period when he played a delightful one-two with substitute Kyle Lafferty before rifling home an unstoppable rising strike. Kris Boyd then blasted home low and hard from the penalty spot after Kenny Miller had been fouled in the box. Right at the end, Miller himself scored – after being set up by Kevin Thomson – to complete a fine afternoon's work.

Incidentally, Steven Whittaker (10 goals in all competitions) was now the first Rangers defender for more than 40 years to reach double figures in a season.

With the game in Perth against St Johnstone cancelled due to a frozen pitch, Rangers then had a free weekend before facing Celtic in the third Old Firm clash of the campaign. Both Allan McGregor and Artur Boruc were in fine form and the game seemed to be heading for a 0-0 conclusion after the Celtic keeper made another fine save from a Sasa Papac drive right at the end. From the resultant corner and subsequent goalmouth melee, however, substitute Maurice Edu poked home from close range (after both Madjid Bougherra and Kris Boyd had been denied by Boruc) to secure the points for Rangers with virtually the last kick of the game. Just days after his 62nd birthday, Walter Smith had matched the 26 derby wins achieved by former Old Firm managers Scot Symon (Rangers) and Jock Stein (Celtic).

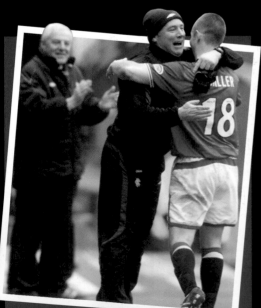

MARCH

Although fellow Co-operative Insurance Cup finalists St Mirren took the lead at Ibrox – through on-loan Celtic defender Graham Carey's super free-kick – Lee McCulloch netted either side of half-time to put Rangers in front with a well-taken double. Substitute Nacho Novo added a third in the closing minutes with a near-post finish from a Steven Davis free-kick as the Light Blues recorded their second 3-1 league win of the season. During the game, Davis, Sasa Papac and DaMarcus Beasley also came close to scoring but were denied by the woodwork on each occasion.

Rangers moved 13 points clear in the championship race following a 2-0 win at Rugby Park against Kilmarnock three days later. After an evenly-balanced first period, second half goals from Steven Whittaker (drilling a headed clearance high into the net) and Kenny Miller (firing home after keeper Bell blocked from Steven Davis) secured a crucial win prior to a short league break for the Active Nation Scottish Cup and the Co-operative Insurance Cup final.

At Tynecastle against Hearts, Rangers earned a stunning 4-1 victory after exiting the Active Nation Scottish Cup earlier that week. Youngster Danny Wilson, with his first goal for the Club, set the ball rolling when he headed past MacDonald following Kevin Thomson's delivery to the far post. Although Santana equalized, Kenny Miller restored Rangers lead when he reacted quickly and cleverly to head home after a Steven Naismith volley came thundering off the crossbar. Naismith (playing in the centre of midfield) would not be denied a goal however and, after the break, hit a double. His first of the game was a delightful chip over the advancing keeper to take advantage of Steven Whittaker's defence-splitting pass into the area. Then, after a Steven Davis free-kick, his precise penalty box header confirmed number two for him and number four for Rangers.

Walter Smith's players then featured in another 4-1 away game but this time as losers at McDiarmid Park. St Johnstone, chasing a top six finish, went two ahead early-on before Sasa Papac pulled one back for the Light Blues. A subsequent deflection off Lee McCulloch confirmed a 3-1 advantage for the Perth side at the break as the rain swirled and the winds bit. Although Rangers created chances in the second period, substitute Murray Davidson made it 4-1 near the end. This was the first time that Rangers had lost more than one goal in the league all season but proved only to be a minor blip in the race for the SPL title.

APRIL

Hamilton Academical, undefeated in six league games, provided another stern test for the league leaders on Heroes and Legends day at Ibrox when Rangers stars of old gathered on the park at half-time. By this stage, the only goal of the game had already been scored. Maurice Edu, who moments earlier smacked the base of the post with a thunderous drive from 25 yards, claimed the winner after steering home from a clever Kenny Miller pass across the penalty area. Rangers now required another three victories to be certain of retaining the championship crown.

Four days later that total was reduced by one following a 3-1 win over Aberdeen at Ibrox. Steven Davis, with an outstanding piece of skill, scored the only goal of the first half when he hit a sumptuous bending drive from 20 yards out that flew past Langfield and soared high into the net. Into the second period, fellow countryman Kyle Lafferty doubled Rangers advantage with another fine solo effort after driving at the red rearguard and thumping home also from distance. Although the visitors then pulled one back, Kenny Miller's hook shot from a Danny Wilson knock down fifteen minutes before the end ensured a comfortable finish to the game.

Next port of call was Tannadice and a game against Active Nation Scottish Cup finalists Dundee United in the last match before the league split. Although the Light Blues had the better of the chances –

Kenny Miller came close with a dipping volley in the first half and a shot that came back off the inside of the post late in the second period – the game ended 0-0. This was only the fifth time that Rangers had failed to score in the league this season.

Back in Glasgow against Hearts, Kyle Lafferty scored for a second successive home game when his bullet header (from a Kevin Thomson corner early in the second period) ripped past MacDonald in goal. Kenny Miller then blasted home from the penalty spot for his 20th goal of the season as Rangers moved closer to the SPL title following a 2-0 win. Between them, strikers Miller and Kris Boyd had now amassed a 44 goal total for the Club this season.

With one more victory required to ensure championship celebrations, it was unfortunate that due to the demolition of the old East Stand at Easter Road, only 1500 Rangers fans could be accommodated for the match against Hibernian in Edinburgh. They did make their presence felt however! Kyle Lafferty, following a Kenny Miller lofted ball, scored the only goal of the game when he held off McCormack and then Hogg before firing home across the keeper with an angled left foot shot. Walter Smith's side – only two league defeats and unbeaten domestically at Ibrox – had achieved back-to-back SPL titles with three games to spare. A special word of praise is reserved for Club captain David Weir who, just short of his 40th birthday, played every minute of every SPL game on the road to glory.

MAY

Walter Smith made several changes for the trip to Tannadice to face Dundee United but Rangers still played like Champions, especially in a first half of sustained pressure. Kris Boyd, with his 100th SPL goal for the Club, opened the scoring right at the start of the game when he coolly buried past Pernis following John Fleck's perfectly judged through-ball. Nacho Novo then doubled the visitors' tally just before the break with a low drive beyond the keeper. Although the home side pulled one back in the second period, Rangers dominated much more than the final 2-1 score would suggest.

Lee Naylor's deflected free-kick gave Celtic an early lead in the final Old Firm encounter of the league campaign. Although Kenny Miller equalised with a super header late in the first period, Fortune restored the home side's advantage just before the break.

Rangers pushed hard throughout the second period and, after creating several openings, were somewhat unfortunate not to draw level before the final whistle.

First half goals from Kris Boyd and Kyle Lafferty put Rangers in front against Motherwell at Ibrox on the last day of the 2009/10 SPL season. Although the visitors pulled one back just after the break, Lafferty scored again for a 3-1 advantage to the Champions. However, right at the end, Craig Brown's side scored twice – once from the penalty spot – to level at 3-3. The disappointment of losing two late goals was soon forgotten however when David Weir was presented with the SPL championship trophy at the end of the game as players and fans alike celebrated another quite remarkable chapter in the history of Rangers Football Club.

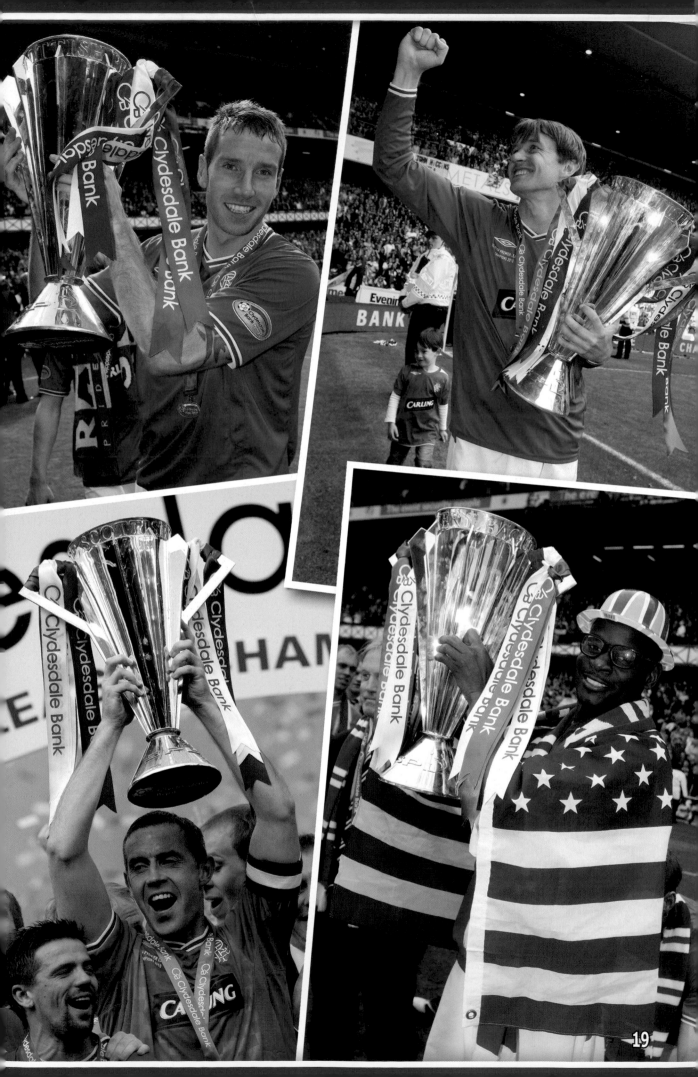

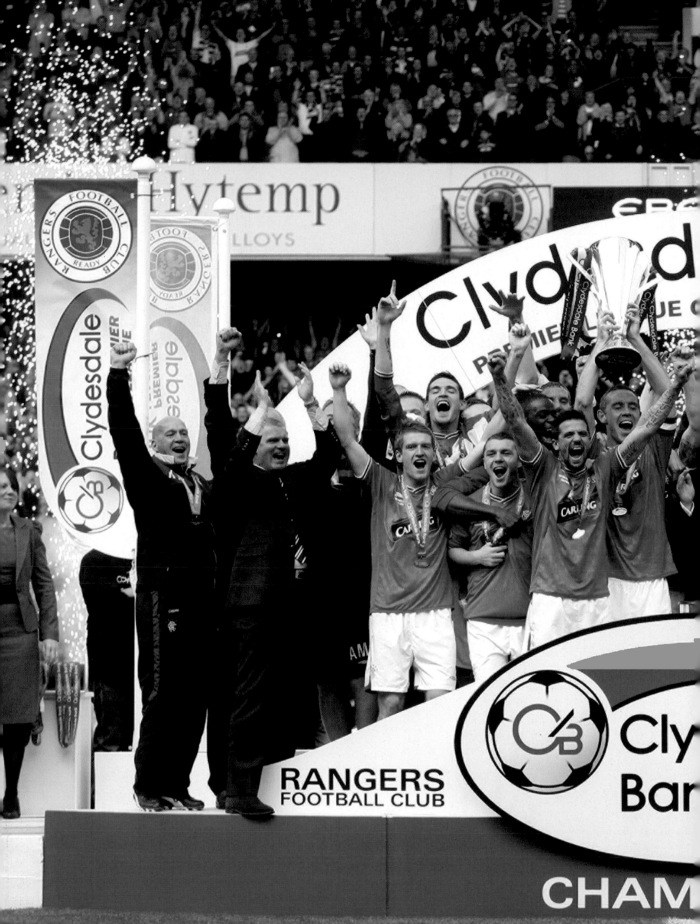

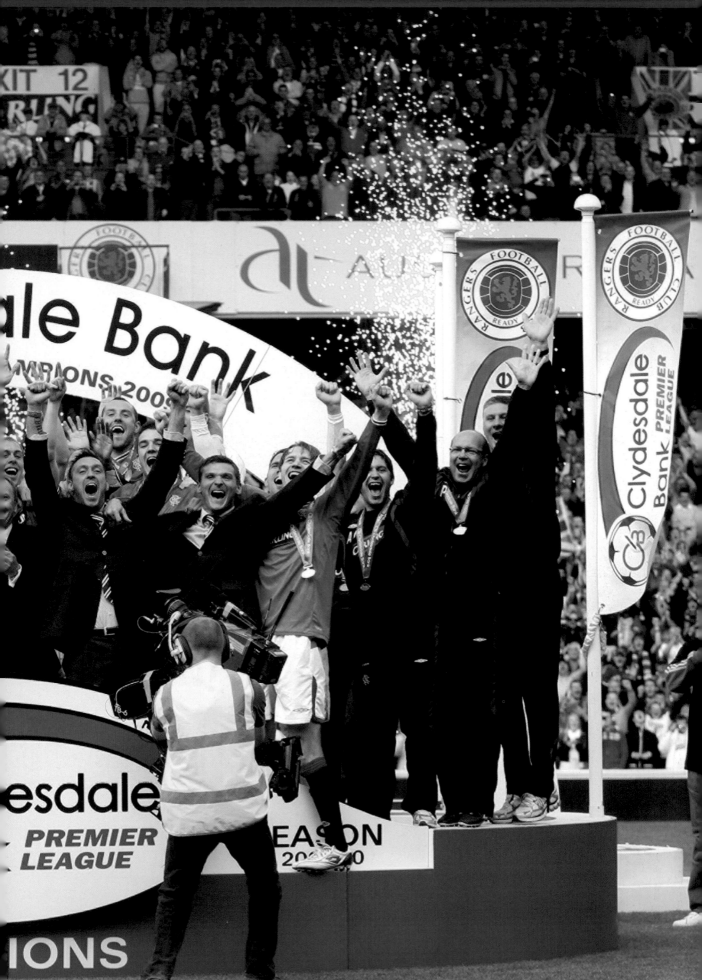

21

Allan McGregor

BORN:	Edinburgh, Scotland
DATE OF BIRTH:	31.01.1982
HEIGHT:	1.85m (6ft 1in)
WEIGHT:	87 kg (11st 9lbs)
POSITION:	Goalkeeper
SENIOR CAREER:	St Johnstone, (2004 loan), Dunfermline Athletic (2005 loan)
SIGNED FOR RANGERS:	Product of Rangers Youth Team
SEASON 2009/10 FIRST TEAM APPEARANCES:	SPL 34 (0) Scottish Cup 6 (0) Co-operative Insurance Cup 0 (0) UEFA Champions League 6 (0)

Neil Alexander

BORN:	Edinburgh, Scotland
DATE OF BIRTH:	10.03.1978
HEIGHT:	1.85m (6ft 1in)
WEIGHT:	73 kg (11st 7lbs)
POSITION:	Goalkeeper
SENIOR CAREER:	Stenhousemuir (1996-98), Livingston (1998-2001), Cardiff City (2001-07), Ipswich Town (2007-08)
SIGNED FOR RANGERS:	January 2008
SEASON 2009/10 FIRST TEAM APPEARANCES:	SPL 4 (1) Scottish Cup 0 (0) Co-operative Insurance Cup 4 (0) UEFA Champions League 0 (0)

Steven Whittaker

BORN:	Edinburgh, Scotland
DATE OF BIRTH:	16.06.1984
HEIGHT:	1.85m (6ft 1in)
WEIGHT:	81 kg (13st 9lbs)
POSITION:	Defender
SENIOR CAREER:	Hibernian (2002-07)
SIGNED FOR RANGERS:	August 2007
SEASON 2009/10 FIRST TEAM APPEARANCES:	SPL 32 (3) Scottish Cup 5 (0) Co-operative Insurance Cup 4 (0) UEFA Champions League 6 (0)
GOALS:	11

Sasa Papac

BORN:	Mostar, Bosnia
DATE OF BIRTH:	07.02.1980
HEIGHT:	1.85m (6ft 1in)
WEIGHT:	79 kg (12st 4lbs)
POSITION:	Defender
SENIOR CAREER:	FC Karnten (2001-04), Austria Vienna (2004-06)
SIGNED FOR RANGERS:	August 2006
SEASON 2009/10 FIRST TEAM APPEARANCES:	SPL 34 (0) Scottish Cup 4 (0) Co-operative Insurance Cup 3 (0) UEFA Champions League 6 (0)
GOALS:	2

David Weir

BORN:	Falkirk, Scotland
DATE OF BIRTH:	10.05.1970
HEIGHT:	1.89m (6ft 3ins)
WEIGHT:	88 kg (13st 7lbs)
POSITION:	Defender
SENIOR CAREER:	Falkirk (1992-96), Hearts (1996-99), Everton (1999 – 2007)
SIGNED FOR RANGERS:	January 2007
SEASON 2009/10 FIRST TEAM APPEARANCES:	SPL 38 (0) Scottish Cup 5 (0) Co-operative Insurance Cup 3 (0) UEFA Champions League 5 (0)

Madjid Bougherra

BORN:	Dijon, France
DATE OF BIRTH:	07.10.1982
HEIGHT:	1.88m (6ft 2ins)
WEIGHT:	89 kg (14st)
POSITION:	Defender
SENIOR CAREER:	Gueugnon (2002-06), Crewe Alexandra (2006 loan), Sheffield Wednesday (2006-07), Charlton Athletic (2007-08)
SIGNED FOR RANGERS:	August 2008
SEASON 2009/10 FIRST TEAM APPEARANCES:	SPL 16 (1) Scottish Cup 2 (0) Co-operative Insurance Cup 1 (0) UEFA Champions League 3 (0)
GOALS:	2

Kirk Broadfoot

BORN:	Irvine, Scotland
DATE OF BIRTH:	08.08.1984
HEIGHT:	1.87m (6ft 3ins)
WEIGHT:	80 kg (14st)
POSITION:	Defender
SENIOR CAREER:	St Mirren (2002-07)
SIGNED FOR RANGERS:	July 2007
SEASON 2009/10 FIRST TEAM APPEARANCES:	SPL 12 (0) Scottish Cup 3 (1) Co-operative Insurance Cup 0 (0) UEFA Champions League 0 (0)

Andy Webster

BORN:	Dundee, Scotland
DATE OF BIRTH:	23.04.1982
HEIGHT:	1.82m (6ft)
WEIGHT:	84 kg (10st)
POSITION:	Defender
SENIOR CAREER:	Arbroath (1999-2001), Hearts (2001-06), Wigan Athletic (2006-08), Rangers (2007 loan), Rangers (2008 –), Bristol City (2008 loan), Dundee United (2009 loan)
SIGNED FOR RANGERS:	June 2008

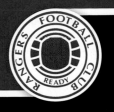

Walter Smith
— The Trophies

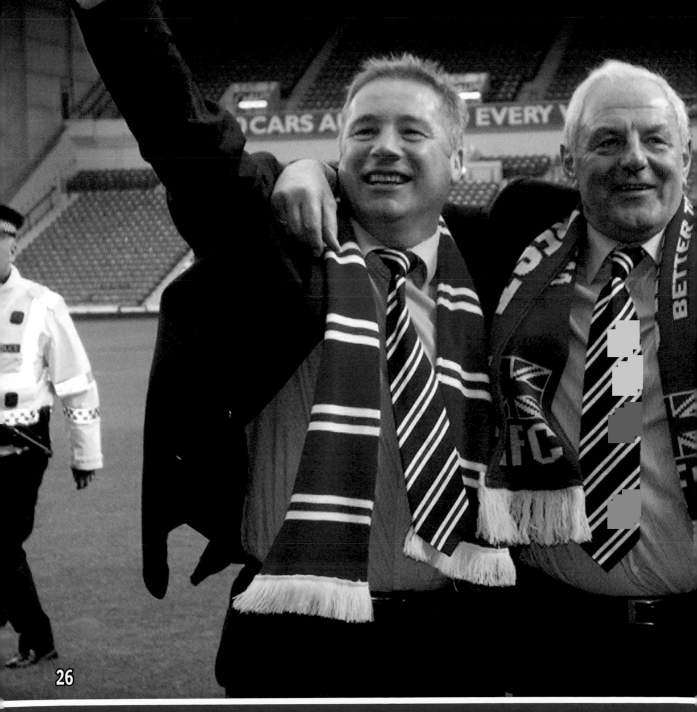

Rangers fans everywhere were naturally delighted when, in late May 2010, Walter Smith confirmed that he would continue as Manager until the end of Season 2010/11. To date, during his two spells in charge, he has guided the Club to a total of 19 domestic trophies.

Premier League Season 1990/91:
Won by two points from Aberdeen

Premier League Season 1991/92:
Won by nine points from Hearts

Scottish Cup Season 1991/92:
Final – Rangers 2 Airdrie 1

Premier League Season 1992/93:
Won by nine points from Aberdeen

League Cup Season 1992/93:
Final – Rangers 2 Aberdeen 1 (AET)

Scottish Cup Season 1992/93:
Final – Rangers 2 Aberdeen 1

Premier League Season 1993/94:
Won by eight points from Aberdeen

League Cup Season 1993/94:
Final – Rangers 2 Hibernian 1

Premier League Season 1994/95:
Won by fifteen points from Motherwell

Premier League Season 1995/96:
Won by four points from Celtic

Scottish Cup Season 1995/96:
Final – Rangers 5 Hearts 1

Premier League Season 1996/97:
Won by five points from Celtic

League Cup Season 1996/97:
Final – Rangers 4 Hearts 3

League Cup Season 2007/08:
Final – Rangers 2 Dundee United 2
(Rangers won after a penalty shoot-out)

Scottish Cup Season 2007/08:
Final – Rangers 3 Queen of the South 2

Premier League Season 2008/09:
Won by four points from Celtic

Scottish Cup Season 2008/09:
Final – Rangers 1 Falkirk 0

League Cup Season 2009/10:
Final – Rangers 1 St Mirren 0

Premier League Season 2009/10:
Won by six points from Celtic
(with three games to play)

ALLY McCOIST –
355 GOALS FOR RANGERS

Ally McCoist scored an incredible 355 goals for Rangers – a Club record. He began his professional career with St Johnstone and, indeed, scored his first goal at Ibrox when the Perth side lost a Scottish Cup tie 3-1 in February 1981. Then, after two years with Sunderland, Rangers manager John Greig agreed a fee in the region of £185,000 to bring the striker back to Scotland in 1983.

For eight of the ten seasons from 1983/84 to 1992/93, he was leading scorer at Rangers and claimed a high of 34 league goals in 1986/87, 1991/92 and 1992/93. On the last day of the 1991/92 period, Ally scored not only his 200th Scottish league goal but also Rangers 100th of the campaign when Aberdeen fell 2-0 at Pittodrie. One of only three players to feature in all 9 in a Row league titles, McCoist also won a record nine League Cup medals and scored a Club record 54 goals in the competition.

His Ibrox career also realised 27 goals in Old Firm fixtures (a total only bettered by RC Hamilton's 36 goals) with hat tricks against the team in green in the 1984 League Cup final and the 1986 Glasgow Cup final. Rangers won both games 3-2. Also worth recalling is a famous night in March 1992 when ten men in light blue defied the elements of a Glasgow monsoon and a Celtic onslaught to reach the Scottish Cup final. The only goal of the game had Ally's name on it.

Away from the domestic arena, his 21 goals in European competition is also an Ibrox record. Few fans will ever forget the diving header that finally silenced Elland Road when Rangers claimed a headline-grabbing 2-1 victory against Leeds United in the European Cup tie of November 1992. A bad leg break playing for Scotland in Portugal in April 1993 put McCoist out of the game for several months. He fought his way back to fitness however and, after appearing as a substitute against Hibernian in the League Cup final of October 1993, he hit the winner with an audacious overhead kick.

'Super Ally' won many individual awards throughout his long and illustrious Rangers career of fifteen years and 581 games. One of these was the prestigious European Golden Boot trophy at the end of Season 1991/92. Twelve months later, after scoring 34 goals in just 34 league games, he became the first player to retain the trophy.

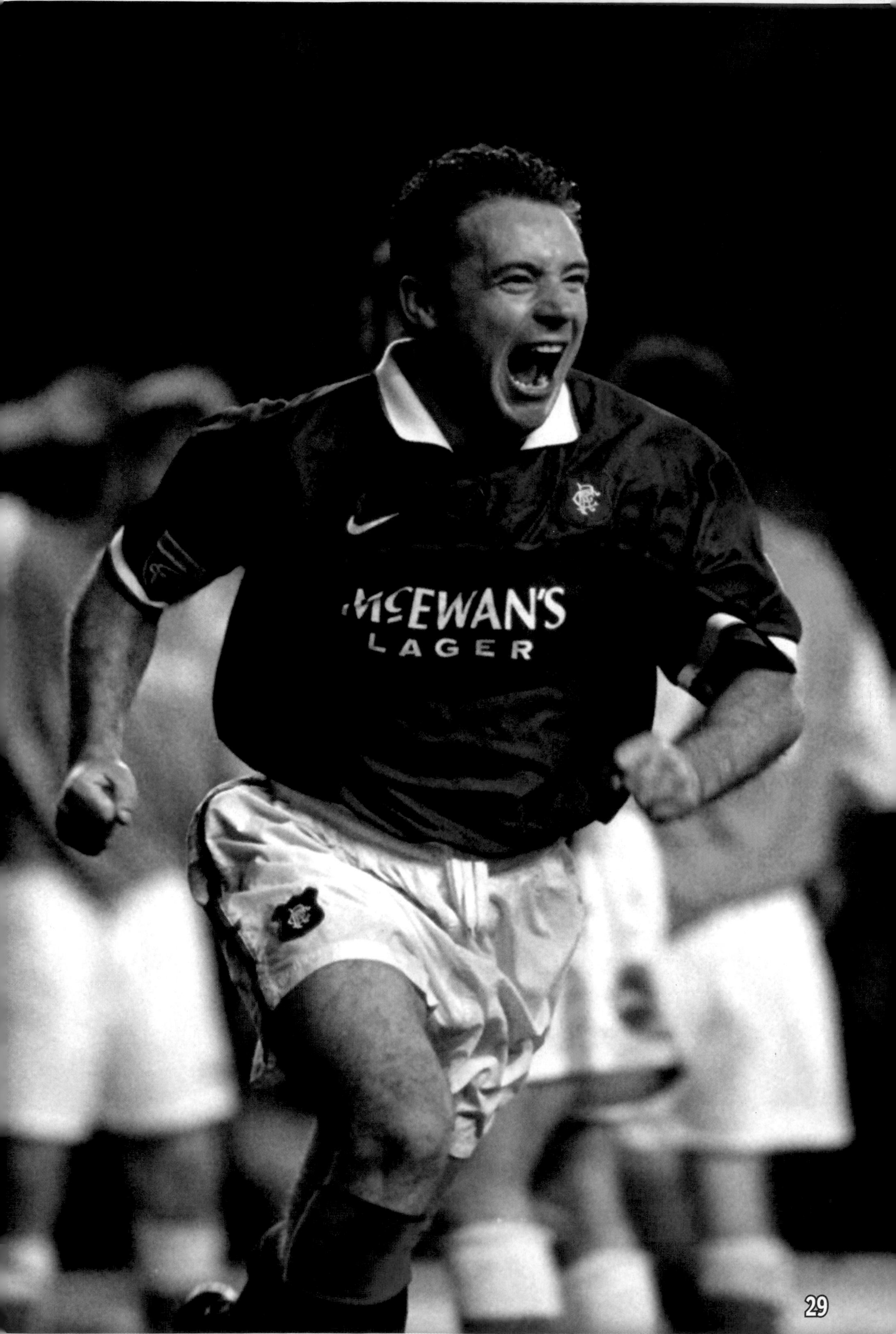
McEWAN'S
LAGER

Mark Hateley –
115 Goals For Rangers

Mark Hateley first arrived at Rangers for the start of Season 1990/91 after three years with Monaco where he won a French championship. Earlier in his career, following a successful 1983/84 period at Portsmouth, the striker famously joined AC Milan in Italy for three seasons.

Although his first year in Glasgow produced ten league goals – including Rangers first of the league campaign in the 3-1 home win over Dunfermline – it was his sensational double on the last day of the season that grabbed the headlines. For that game, Aberdeen came south to Ibrox in the knowledge that a draw would be enough to secure the title. On a day of high emotion, however, Hateley scored both goals in the famous 2-0 win to confirm number three of 9 in a Row for the Club. His first strike that afternoon – a fifteen yard header after soaring high above the red rearguard – is now legendary.

The striker began the next campaign with a hat trick against St Johnstone (6-0, 10/08/1991) before netting another memorable double in the 2-0 Old Firm win at Celtic Park later in August. On the last day of the season, he opened the scoring against Airdrie at Hampden when Rangers lifted the Scottish Cup for the first time since 1981. Between them, in Season 1991/92, Hateley and Ally McCoist scored 55 league goals with 21 and 34 each respectively.

Season 1992/93 (29 goals in total) produced a seemingly endless list of highlights – the magnificent left foot volley from 25 yards against Leeds in the European Cup that screamed past Lukic in goal; the inch-perfect curling cross for Ally's diving header and goal number two in the same away game; Mark's own headed equaliser against Marseille at Ibrox that virtually raised the stadium roof and the superb run and low shot from an acute angle for Rangers second and decisive Scottish Cup final goal.

Hateley was voted Player of the Year for Season 1993/94 by the Scottish Football Writers' Association, becoming the first Englishman to win this award. That season, he was top scorer at the Club with 30 goals. After joining Queens Park Rangers in 1995, the player, answering an injury crisis, returned to Rangers in March 1997 for a short period on the final leg of the 9 in a Row journey. Asked about how he felt coming back to Ibrox, his response was emphatic – 'Coming back? No, I'm coming home!'

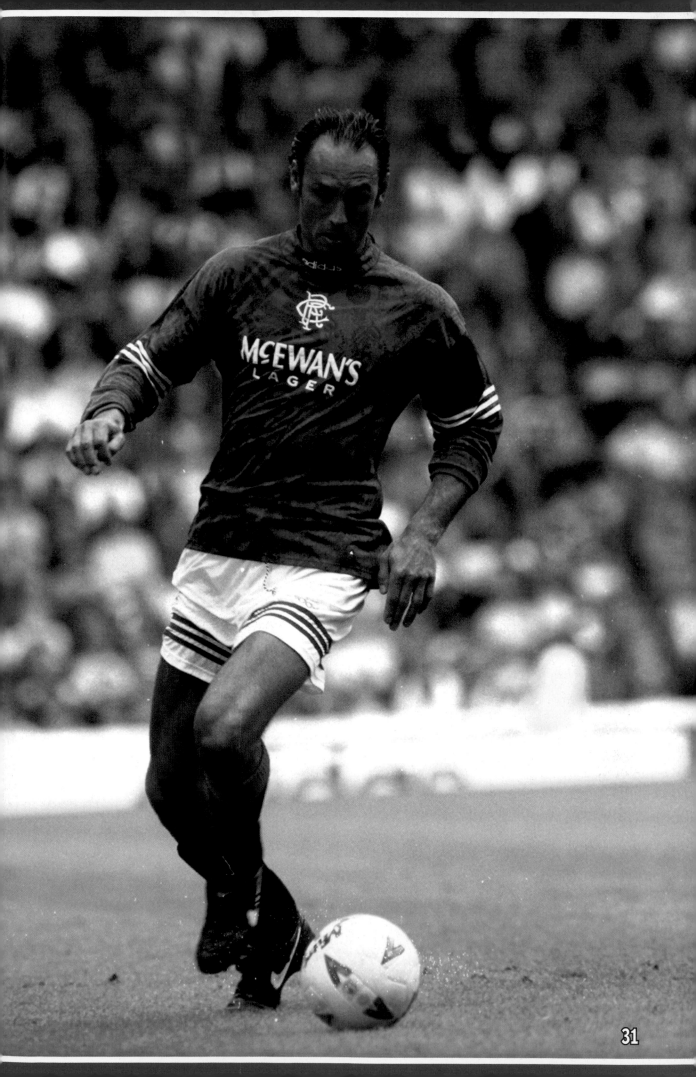

HEADLINE NEWS

**Rangers made the following headlines last season.
What was the occasion?**

Answers on page 60

1 Allan Answers Red Alert
Mail On Sunday, 13.09.09

2 It's a Kind of Madjid
Daily Mail, 17. 09.09

3 HATS OFF TO THE STRIKERS
Mail On Sunday, 20.12.09

4 160!
Daily Mail, 31.12.09

5 Allan Enjoys a Last Laugh
Daily Mail, 4.01.10

6 Little means so much to Walter
Mail On Sunday, 24.01.10

7 Magic Moment
The Sun, 01.03.10

8 MILLER'S MAGIC DEFIES ODDS
Daily Mail, 22.03.10

9 Kyle savours the last laff
Daily Mail, 26.04.10

Season 2009/10 Quiz

Answers on page 60

1   Who scored Rangers first goal on the road to championship glory?

2   Rangers played three league games in September last season. How many ended in victory?

3   In the absence of David Weir, who captained the side when Rangers met Dundee in the 4th round of the Co-operative Insurance Cup?

4   Who scored for Rangers in the SPL at Celtic Park?

5   Rangers recorded both 6-1 and 7-1 wins in the league. Name their opponents.

6   How many goals did defender Steven Whittaker score in the 2009/10 campaign?

7   When Rangers won the championship at Easter Road, only one player had started and finished every league game. Can you name him?

8   How many points separated Rangers and Celtic following the derby game at Ibrox in March?

9   Can you name the substitute whose very late equaliser against Hearts at Ibrox in January maintained the side's unbeaten home record in the league?

10   How many times have Rangers been crowned League Champions?

The Co-operative Insurance Cup 2009/10

The first action in the Co-operative Insurance Cup was an away tie against First Division Queen of the South. The last time Rangers visited Palmerston Park was back in August 1983 when a certain Ally McCoist scored his first-ever goal for the Club in a 4-1 League Cup win. Watching from the dugout on this occasion, the Assistant Manager saw Steven Naismith open the scoring early-on (after Kris Boyd delivered an inch perfect pass across goal) before substitute Nacho Novo doubled Rangers tally late in the second period with a delightful solo effort. In injury time, local hero Bob Harris netted for the home side with a superb strike to confirm a final score of 2-1.

Walter Smith's side then headed in the opposite direction and north to Dens Park for a quarter final date with First Division leaders Dundee. Youngsters Danny Wilson and Jordan McMillan were both handed debuts and Sasa Papac was Captain in the absence of David Weir. Although Jocky Scott's side started well, Rangers took the lead when Steven Whittaker flicked home a header following John Fleck's corner. However, a superb Leigh Griffiths free kick restored parity before the break. Into the second period, defender MacKenzie headed past Bullock for an own goal before Nacho Novo set up Fleck who slotted home to make it 3-1 on the night.

Following goals against St Mirren and Falkirk in the previous two (league) games, midfielder Steven Davis made it 3 in a row when he scored Rangers opener in the semi-final clash with St Johnstone at a snowy Hampden. Although keeper Smith did well to save the Ulsterman's initial flick shot following Nacho Novo's near post ball, he was helpless when Davis volleyed home after the ball spun up in the air. Later in the first half, Lee McCulloch made it 2-0 when his controlled drive from the edge of the area found the net through an area crowded with players. This victory meant that Walter Smith had now guided Rangers to an impressive five consecutive domestic cup finals since his return to the Club.

Final opponents St Mirren disposed of fellow SPL sides Kilmarnock, Motherwell and Hearts on the way to the first major cup final in 23 years for the Paisley outfit. Gus MacPherson's side started the game really well and, indeed, dominated a scoreless first half. After the break, the odds on a Rangers victory were greatly reduced following the dismissals of both Kevin Thomson and Danny Wilson. The nine men

in blue defied the odds however and minutes from the end Kenny Miller wrote his name in the history books with a superb winning goal. Following a swift counter-attack and pinpoint cross into the box from wide right by substitute Steven Naismith, the Scotland striker headed precisely and perfectly into the bottom corner past the outstretched fingertips of keeper Gallacher. Miller's goal earned Rangers their 26th League Cup triumph in another stunning season for the Club.

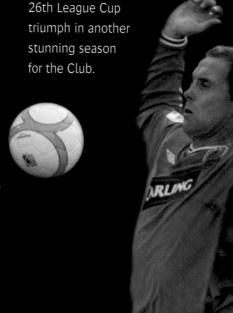

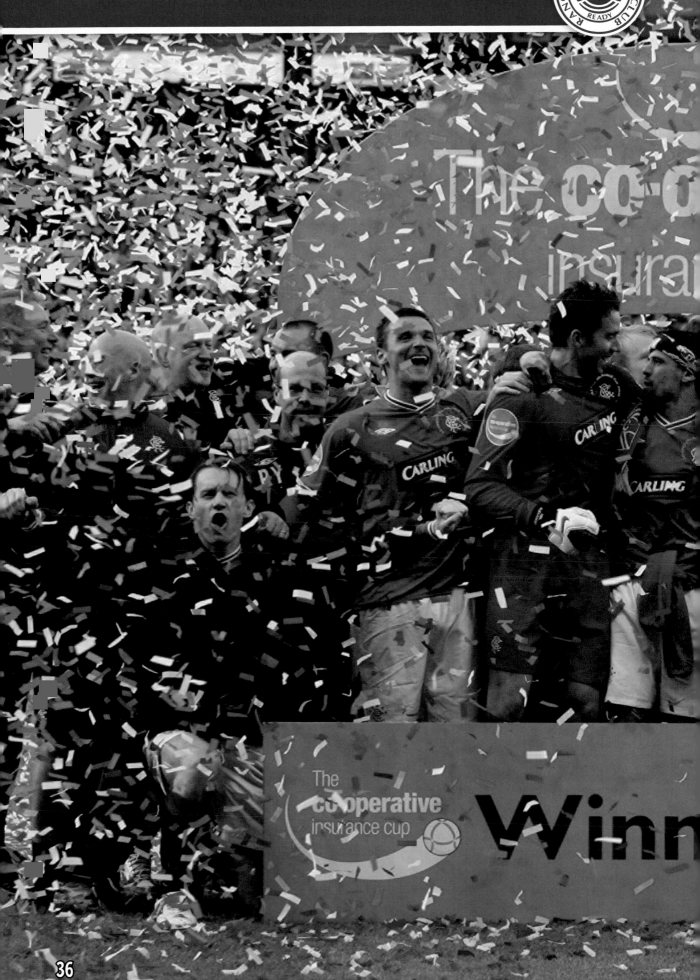

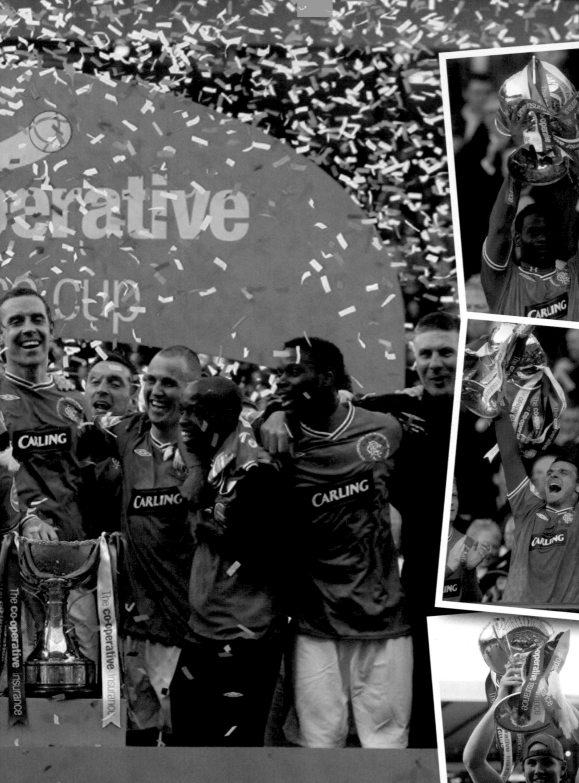

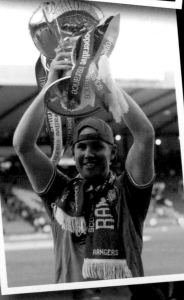

The 26 League Cup Winning Finals

Season 1946/47   Rangers 4 Aberdeen 0
Goals from Jimmy Duncanson (2), Torry Gillick and Billy Williamson won the final of the inaugural League Cup tournament. Although 134,000 tickets were sold, the actual attendance was 82,684 due to the appalling (April) weather!

Season 1948/49   Rangers 2 Raith Rovers 0
Part one of Scotland's first-ever domestic treble of League Cup, Scottish Cup and League Championship. Torry Gillick and Willie Paton scored against Division B side Raith Rovers.

Season 1960/61   Rangers 2 Kilmarnock 0
Ralph Brand claimed a hat-trick in the 7-0 semi-final win over Queen of the South. The striker also netted in the final along with winger Alex Scott.

Season 1961/62   Rangers 1 Hearts 1
Rangers 3 Hearts 1
Following an even first (October) game, Rangers turned on the style in the (December) replay. Although Jimmy Millar, Ralph Brand and Ian McMillan got the goals, Jim Baxter was the team's inspiration.

Season 1963/64   Rangers 5 Morton 0
Cousins Jim Forrest and Alec Willoughby were the day's heroes – claiming all five goals between them. Forrest netted four times to establish a cup final record by a Rangers player.

Season 1964/65   Rangers 2 Celtic 1
Jim Forrest was again the man of the hour, following-up his two goals in the 2-1 semi-final win over Dundee United with another double against Celtic in the final as Rangers retained the trophy.

Season 1970/71   Rangers 1 Celtic 0
Victory over Celtic again, this time courtesy of
sixteen-year-old Derek Johnstone's famous headed
goal from a Willie Johnston cross.
This was the Club's first major trophy in
four years.

Season 1975/76   Rangers 1 Celtic 0
Light Blue legend John Greig lifted the trophy
for the first time as Captain following Alex
MacDonald's flying header in the Old Firm final.
Rangers also completed the domestic treble.

Season 1977/78   Rangers 2 Celtic 1
Extra-time was required to defeat Celtic this time.
Goals by Gordon Smith and Davie Cooper confirmed
part one of another domestic treble triumph – the
Club's second in three years.

Season 1978/79   Rangers 2 Aberdeen 1
This was John Greig's first trophy as Manager of the
Club. Although Aberdeen led for most of the game,
goals from Alex MacDonald and centre-half Colin
Jackson sealed victory.

Season 1981/82   Rangers 2 Dundee United 1
Once again Rangers came from behind and late
goals by Davie Cooper and Ian Redford saved the day.
Incidentally, both strikes were from twenty yards.

Season 1983/84   Rangers 3 Celtic 2
Just like the last Old Firm League Cup final, extra-time
was required to confirm the destination of the trophy.
Ally McCoist did all the damage with a hat-trick.

Season 1984/85   Rangers 1 Dundee United 0
Iain Ferguson, signed from Dundee at the start of the
campaign, claimed the only goal of the game on a
skidding Hampden surface in atrocious wet conditions.

Season 1986/87   Rangers 2 Celtic 1
Ian Durrant and Davie Cooper (with a late penalty
conversion) gave Graeme Souness his first major
trophy as Manager of Rangers.

Season 1987/88   Rangers 3 Aberdeen 3
(Rangers won after a penalty shoot-out)
This was one of the great finals of the competition.
Aberdeen led 3-2 before Robert Fleck's late equalizer
meant extra-time and, subsequently, penalties. Ian
Durrant scored the decisive spot kick.

Season 1988/89   Rangers 3 Aberdeen 2
Ally McCoist's last minute goal – his second of the
game – ensured that the trophy was Ibrox bound
for a third successive year. This was the first time
Rangers had achieved this feat.

Season 1990/91   Rangers 2 Celtic 1
Despite going behind, a Mark Walters goal took the game into extra-time before Richard Gough hit a stunning winner.

Season 1992/93   Rangers 2 Aberdeen 1
Although Stuart McCall opened the scoring, it was an extra-time own goal by Aberdeen defender Gary Smith that eventually decided the winners of the competition.

Season 1993/94   Rangers 2 Hibernian 1
Substitute Ally McCoist's spectacular overhead strike won the cup after Ian Durrant claimed Rangers first of the game. The final was played at Celtic Park as Hampden was under reconstruction.

Season 1996/97   Rangers 4 Hearts 3
Two goals apiece by Paul Gascoigne and Ally McCoist settled the outcome on the coldest of November days when Celtic Park was once again the venue.

Season 1998/99   Rangers 2 St Johnstone 1
This was the last season in which the competition was completed in the autumn. Frenchman Stephane Guivarc'h and German Jorg Albertz both scored for Rangers.

Season 2001/02   Rangers 4 Ayr United 0
Alex McLeish's first trophy as Manager of Rangers and Barry Ferguson's first as Captain of the Club. Tore Andre Flo, Ferguson and Claudio Caniggia (2) all scored on cup final day against First Division opponents.

Season 2002/03   Rangers 2 Celtic 1
Despite sustained Celtic pressure in the second period, first half goals from Claudio Caniggia and Peter Lovenkrands secured part one of a domestic treble.

Season 2004/05   Rangers 5 Motherwell 1
Defenders Maurice Ross and Sotirios Kyrgiakos both scored with less than ten minutes played before Fernando Ricksen, Nacho Novo and Kyrgiakos (again) completed the rout.

Season 2007/08   Rangers 2 Dundee United 2
(Rangers won after a penalty shoot-out)
Dundee United led twice before substitute Kris Boyd leveled twice in a dramatic final. Boyd then scored with the very last spot kick to secure victory 3-2 on penalties.

Season 2009/10   Rangers 1 St Mirren 0
Kenny Miller headed the winner for nine-man Rangers on a day of high drama at Hampden.

Goal of the Season

Kenny Miller v St Mirren

Co-operative Insurance Cup final
Hampden, March 2010

In build-up and execution, this was a goal of real quality. With Rangers down to nine men and extra-time looming, David Weir began a swift counter-attack and fed substitute Steven Naismith wide right as Kenny Miller and Nacho Novo sprinted through the middle. The former Kilmarnock player then delivered a pinpoint cross to Miller whose perfect penalty box header found the bottom corner of the net just beyond the keeper's outstretched fingertips.

Who Said That Last Season?

1 "Can I not just play Old Firm games every week?"

2 "He has been terrific for us, easily our most consistent player in the last couple of seasons."

3 "It was the first time my mum, dad and two brothers had all been over for a game so I wanted to celebrate (my goal) but I couldn't really because we needed to try to get a second goal for the win."

4 "The way the supporters have taken to him in his six years at the Club is a tribute in itself. There is a great love and genuine warmth from the fans to him."

5 "That goal is up there with the most memorable I've scored. It was fantastic when I netted here against Italy for Scotland but this time I've scored the winner in a cup final."

Answers on page 60

SUMMER SIGNINGS

JAMES BEATTIE

Striker James Beattie joined Rangers for the start of the 2010/11 campaign after a senior career with Blackburn Rovers (1995-98), Southampton (1998-2005), Everton (2005-07), Sheffield United (2007-09) and Stoke City (2009/10).

In January 2005, Everton paid Southampton £6 million for his services - the largest transfer fee the club had ever sanctioned for a player at the time. Beattie was the club's top scorer in his first year on Merseyside with ten Premiership goals. At Sheffield United in Season 2007/08, he became the first player at the club to score from free kicks in three consecutive games. His 22 league goals that year made him joint second highest scorer in the Football League Championship. Back in the Premier League after joining Stoke City in January 2009, the powerful target man scored four times in his first five games for the Britannia Stadium club.

NIKICA JELAVIC

Striker Nikica Jelavic – nicknamed 'The Flying Fortress' because of his heading ability – joined Rangers after two years with Rapid Vienna in the Austrian Bundesliga. In addition to the 18 league goals that he scored throughout the 2009/10 campaign, the 6ft 2in Croatian internationalist also netted nine times in 12 Europa League games for Rapid Vienna. This impressive European tally last season included three goals against Celtic, one against Hamburg and two against Aston Villa.

VLADIMIR WEISS

Winger Vladimir Weiss arrived at the Club on a one-year loan deal from Manchester City and made his Rangers debut after appearing as a second half substitute in the 3-0 win against Hibernian at Easter Road in August. During the 2010 World Cup tournament in South Africa, the Slovakian youngster impressed when he featured for his country against New Zealand, Paraguay and the Netherlands.

PLAYER PROFILES

Lee McCulloch

BORN:	Bellshill, Scotland
DATE OF BIRTH:	14.05.1978
HEIGHT:	1.80m (6ft 1in)
WEIGHT:	78 kg (13st 2lbs)
POSITION:	Midfielder
SENIOR CAREER:	Motherwell (1995-2001), Wigan Athletic (2001-07)
SIGNED FOR RANGERS:	July 2007
SEASON 2009/10 FIRST TEAM APPEARANCES:	SPL 32 (2) Scottish Cup 4 (0) Co-operative Insurance Cup 2 (1) UEFA Champions League 6 (0)
GOALS:	7

Steven Davis

BORN:	Ballymena, Northern Ireland
DATE OF BIRTH:	01.01.1985
HEIGHT:	1.70m (5ft 8ins)
WEIGHT:	67 kg (11st)
POSITION:	Midfielder
SENIOR CAREER:	Aston Villa (2003-07), Fulham (2007-08), Rangers (2008 loan)
SIGNED FOR RANGERS:	August 2008
SEASON 2009/10 FIRST TEAM APPEARANCES:	SPL 36 (0) Scottish Cup 5 (0) Co-operative Insurance Cup 3 (0) UEFA Champions League 6 (0)
GOALS:	4

Maurice Edu

BORN:	California, USA
DATE OF BIRTH:	18.04.1986
HEIGHT:	1.83m (6ft)
WEIGHT:	77 kg (12st 2lbs)
POSITION:	Midfielder
SENIOR CAREER:	Toronto FC (2007-08)
SIGNED FOR RANGERS:	August 2008
SEASON 2009/10 FIRST TEAM APPEARANCES:	SPL 8 (7) Scottish Cup 2 (2) Co-operative Insurance Cup 0 (1) UEFA Champions League 0 (0)
GOALS:	2

Steven Naismith

BORN:	Irvine, Scotland
DATE OF BIRTH:	14.09.1986
HEIGHT:	1.78m (5ft 10ins)
WEIGHT:	72 kg (11st 4lbs)
POSITION:	Striker
SENIOR CAREER:	Kilmarnock (2003-07)
SIGNED FOR RANGERS:	August 2007
SEASON 2009/10 FIRST TEAM APPEARANCES:	SPL 20 (8) Scottish Cup 3 (0) Co-operative Insurance Cup 1 (3) UEFA Champions League 4 (0)
GOALS:	4

John Fleck

BORN:	Glasgow, Scotland
DATE OF BIRTH:	24.08.1991
HEIGHT:	1.75m (5ft 7ins)
WEIGHT:	69 kg (11st 5lbs)
POSITION:	Striker
SENIOR CAREER:	(2007 –)
SIGNED FOR RANGERS:	Product of Rangers Youth Policy
SEASON 2009/10 FIRST TEAM APPEARANCES:	SPL 8 (7) Scottish Cup 2 (1) Co-operative Insurance Cup 2 (0) UEFA Champions League 0 (3)
GOALS:	2

Andrew Little

BORN:	Enniskillen, Northern Ireland
DATE OF BIRTH:	12.05.1989
HEIGHT:	1.84m (6ft)
WEIGHT:	79 kg (12st)
POSITION:	Striker
SENIOR CAREER:	(2007 –)
SIGNED FOR RANGERS:	Product of Rangers Youth Policy
SEASON 2009/10 FIRST TEAM APPEARANCES:	SPL 2 (4) Scottish Cup 1 (2) Co-operative Insurance Cup 0 (1) UEFA Champions League 0 (0)
GOALS:	1

Kyle Lafferty

BORN:	Enniskillen, Northern Ireland
DATE OF BIRTH:	21.07.1987
HEIGHT:	1.93m (6ft 4ins)
WEIGHT:	70 kg (11st)
POSITION:	Striker
SENIOR CAREER:	Burnley (2005 – 08), Darlington (2006 loan)
SIGNED FOR RANGERS:	June 2008
SEASON 2009/10 FIRST TEAM APPEARANCES:	SPL 17 (11) Scottish Cup 4 (1) Co-operative Insurance Cup 2 (0) UEFA Champions League 2 (2)
GOALS:	7

Kenny Miller

BORN:	Edinburgh, Scotland
DATE OF BIRTH:	23.12.1979
HEIGHT:	1.75m (5ft 10ins)
WEIGHT:	67 kg (10st 9lbs)
POSITION:	Striker
SENIOR CAREER:	Hibernian (1998-2000), Stenhousemuir (1998-99 loan), Rangers (2000-01), Wolverhampton Wanderers (2001 loan), Wolverhampton Wanderers 2001-06), Celtic (2006-07), Derby County (2007-08)
SIGNED FOR RANGERS:	June 2000 and June 2008
SEASON 2009/10 FIRST TEAM APPEARANCES:	SPL 29 (4) Scottish Cup 3 (3) Co-operative Insurance Cup 1 (0) UEFA Champions League 5 (0)
GOALS:	21

Memorable Goals from Season 2009/10

Lee McCulloch
Home v Falkirk, August 2009

The first goal on the trail of SPL glory was also one of the best of the Club's league campaign. Midfielder Lee McCulloch, almost 30 yards from goal, hit the sweetest of strikes that rose all the way and screamed into the top corner of the net.

Kenny Miller
Home v Celtic, October 2009

This was the crucial opening goal in the first Old Firm meeting of last season. Following Kris Boyd's defence-splitting pass, strike partner Kenny Miller calmly stroked home past Boruc with a right foot finish.

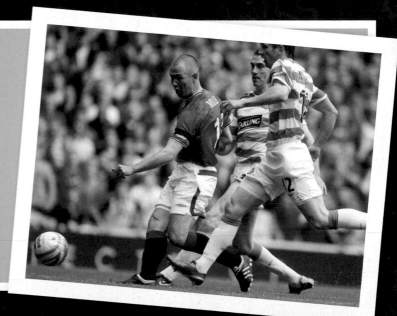

Sasa Papac
Away v St Johnstone, October 2009

With less than ten minutes remaining and the score 1-1, full back Sasa Papac was the surprising match winner when his superb left foot drive from the edge of the penalty box beat veteran stopper Main to ensure full points in Perth.

DaMarcus Beasley
Away v Dundee United, December 2009

USA star DaMarcus Beasley, with his first goal since the 2008 Scottish Cup final, opened the scoring at Tannadice with a stunning left foot shot from the angle of the area that swerved and dipped before finding the far corner of the net.

Kenny Miller
Home v Motherwell, December 2009

On a day when Rangers hit Motherwell for six, Kenny Miller opened Rangers account with a sublime right foot strike from more than 20 yards that sailed over the keeper and into the net via the underside of the crossbar.

Kris Boyd
Home v Dundee United, December 2009

Number three of a first half hat-trick bagged by Kris Boyd inside nine minutes was the goal that equaled the SPL scoring record of 158 held by former Celt Henrik Larsson.

Madjid Bougherra
Home v Dundee United, December 2009

This was a truly special goal. After gaining possession in the centre circle, Madjid Bougherra left one, two, three then four Dundee United players in his wake before sending a powerful left foot shot high into the net.

Lee McCulloch
Away v Celtic, January 2010

Celtic had victory in sight before Lee McCulloch rescued a point for Rangers when his bullet header, from a precise Steven Davis corner, silenced the home support in the east end of Glasgow.

Andrew Little
Home v Hearts, January 2010

With Rangers unbeaten domestic record at Ibrox in real danger, substitute Andrew Little was the stoppage time hero when he guided home from close range after the keeper failed to hold a powerful Lee McCulloch shot.

Steven Whittaker
Home v Hibernian, February 2010

This was Steven Whittaker's 10th goal of 2009/10 and it confirmed his status as the first Rangers defender in over 40 years to reach double figures in a season.

Maurice Edu
Home v Celtic, February 2010

Just before the final whistle, midfielder Maurice Edu bundled home from close range for the only goal of the game as Rangers moved 10 points clear at the top of the league table.

Kenny Miller
Away v Hearts, March 2010

Following a Steven Naismith volley that crashed off the crossbar, Kenny Miller reacted quicker than the home defenders to head home for a 2-1 lead at Tynecastle.

Steven Davis
Home v Aberdeen, April 2010

Steven Davis scored a real gem of a goal when, in the first half, he hit a sumptuous bending drive from 20 yards that flew past the Aberdeen keeper and soared high into the net.

Kenny Miller
Home v Hearts, April 2010

Kenny Miller's 20th goal of the season was a blasted penalty for Rangers second goal of the game.

Kyle Lafferty
Away v Hibernian, April 2010

The goal that finally confirmed the destination of the 2009/10 league title was an assured finish by Kyle Lafferty who fired home across the keeper with an angled left foot strike.

The Active Nation Scottish Cup 2009/10

Rangers joined the 2009/10 Active Nation Scottish Cup at the fourth round stage of the competition and the first obstacle on the road to retaining the trophy was a difficult away tie against Hamilton Academical at New Douglas Park. Initially, the Light Blues seemed to be in control of the tie after strikes from Steven Whittaker (rifling home off the crossbar) and Kenny Miller (steering past the keeper from just inside the box) established a two goal cushion in the first half. Billy Reid's side, however, hit back with a vengeance before the interval and scored three times to take a 3-2 advantage into the break. By this stage, both Steven Davis and Kris Boyd had succumbed to injury. All was not lost though and Kenny Miller netted from the spot in the second period to ensure an Ibrox replay. Incidentally, this was the Scotland striker's fourth double in his last five appearances for the Club.

Although Rangers created numerous opportunities throughout the first ninety minutes of the replay (including two Kenny Miller efforts that hit the crossbar), the tie was eventually decided in the first period of extra-time thanks to two Steven Whittaker goals.

The opener was courtesy of Miller whose superb lofted ball over keeper Cerny was net bound before Whittaker made doubly sure, passing the ball into the empty net. Then, almost immediately, the defender received the ball on the left before cutting inside to fire a bullet shot across the keeper into the far corner. Victory came at a cost however with both Kenny Miller and Nacho Novo hobbling off injured before the final whistle.

The fifth round tie also required two games to decide the winner after Rangers and St Mirren drew the first game 0-0 in Paisley. The Ibrox replay was decided right at the end of the match when, following Steven Smith's long ball to the 18 yard area and Kirk Broadfoot's subsequent head flick, Kris Boyd fired past Gallacher for the only goal of the game and passage into the next round of the tournament.

This quarter-final tie was a Sunday lunchtime TV clash against Dundee United at Ibrox. Although the visitors scored first, goals from Kris Boyd (two first-half penalty conversions) and Nacho Novo (early in the second period) established a 3-1 lead before Peter Houston's side replied twice for a 3-3 final score. The subsequent Tannadice replay – three days after Rangers lifted the Co-operative Insurance Cup – was evenly balanced and seemed destined for extra-time. However, right at the end, the home side snatched a winner when Allan McGregor's block on a Robertson effort ended with the ball ricocheting into the net.

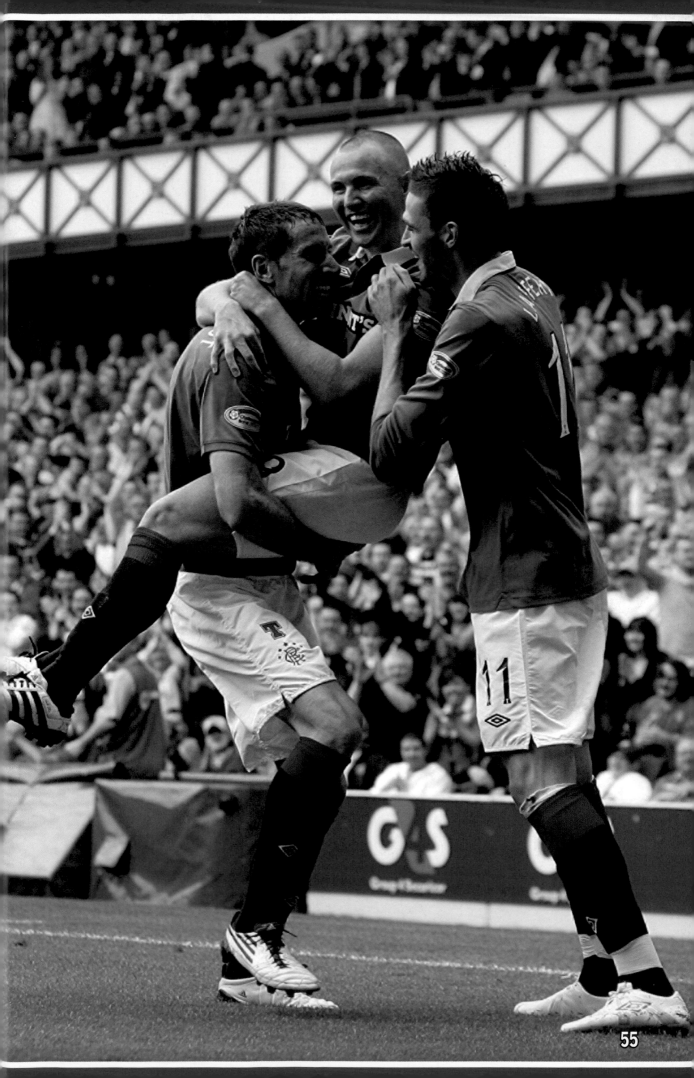

Rangers Annual Player of the Year 2009/10

Striker Kenny Miller returned to Rangers for a second spell with the Club prior to the start of the 2008/09 period and excelled right from the start, forming an impressive partnership with Kris Boyd in attack. Between them, the duo hit the back of the net 44 times that season. Miller scored 13 of those campaign goals including, most memorably in late August, a crucial double in the wonderful 4-2 Old Firm win at Celtic Park. In addition to his own tally, the player was also the architect of numerous other goals for Walter Smith's championship-winning side.

Last season, Miller's contribution to the side was even more impressive. He scored 21 goals in all domestic competitions – 18 in the Scottish Premier League, 2 in the Active Nation Scottish Cup and 1 in the Co-operative Insurance Cup. His double on the opening day of the league campaign against Falkirk was followed by another brace of greater significance in early October when he scored both his side's goals in the 2-1 Old Firm derby win to take Rangers within one point of league leaders Celtic at the top of the SPL table.

In December, the striker netted doubles in three consecutive games when Dundee United (away), Motherwell (home) and Hibernian (away) were put to the sword 3-0, 6-1 and 4-1 respectively. At the National Stadium in late March, Miller's name was also on the goal that decided the destination of the 2009/10 Co-operative Insurance Cup. Weighted to perfection, his astonishingly accurate header for nine man Rangers that Sunday afternoon was one of the great Hampden goals for the Club.

Miller's last goal of 2009/10 was another superbly judged header in the final Old Firm joust of the league campaign. Additionally, his overall attacking performance that night at Celtic Park was also mightily impressive – his pace and powerful running caused problems by the score for the green and white rearguard. Although the league championship was of course already won by this time, his commitment to the Rangers cause was still 100% – just as it had been in every single game from day one of the journey back in August.

Kenny Miller – Rangers Annual Player of the Year for Season 2009/10

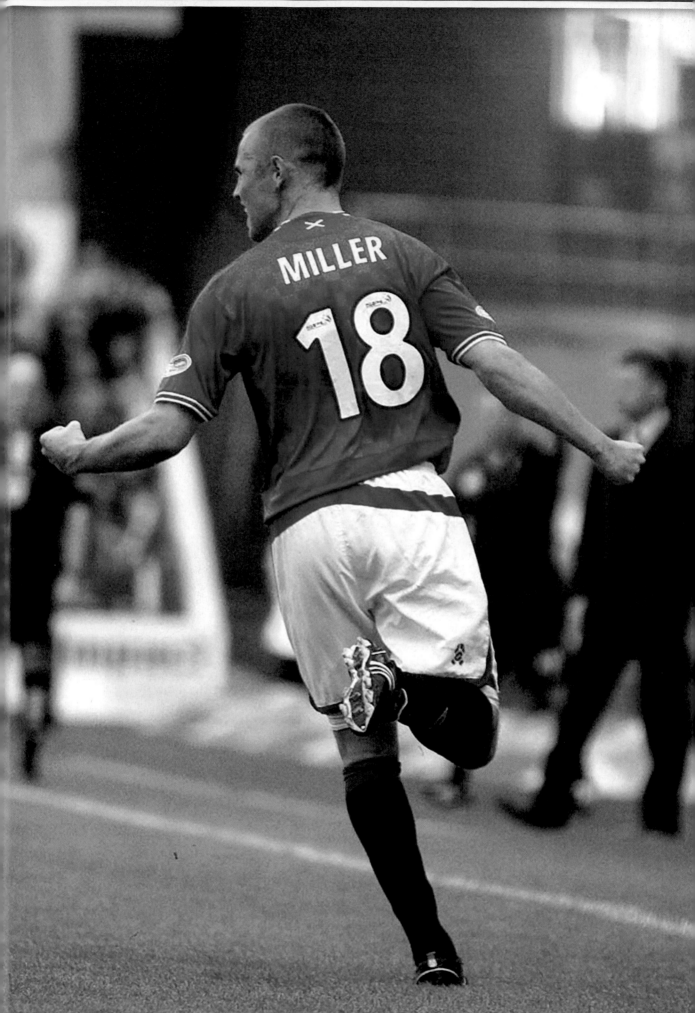

Rangers Young Supporters Club

Join Rangers Young Supporters Club and get closer to all the action at Ibrox!

Rangers Young Supporters Club is an exclusive members only club for Rangers fans aged 16 and under. Being a member is the only way to become a matchday mascot, plus when you join you receive a fantastic membership pack which includes:

Plus, being a member of Rangers Young Supporters Club you are entitled to exclusive benefits including:

MEMBERSHIP BENEFITS
- The chance to be a matchday mascot
- FREE entry to SPL matches with a full paying adult[1]
- 5% discount in JJB stores[2]
- FREE entry to The Ibrox Tour with a full paying adult[3]
- The chance to be selected to take part in exclusive first-team events
- Plus we are always working to get more discounts on fun activities for our fans, visit rangers.co.uk for more information!

MEMBERSHIP PACK
- Rangers bootbag
- Rangers mini football
- Rangers water bottle
- Membership card
- Official certificate
- Birthday card

[1]Games selected by the Club, call the hotline for more information. [2]Discount valid in JJB Rangers stores and JJB stores for Rangers products only. Offer excludes sale items. Only on production of a valid membership card. [3]Excluding school holidays. One tour per member, bookings must be made in advance via the hotline only. ^Calls cost 10ppm from a BT landline, mobile and other providers' charges may vary. *£9.99 season ticket holder price not available from JJB Rangers stores.

Join today, sign up for just £9.99 for juvenile season ticket holders, £15 for UK and £20 for overseas membership!

Rangers Young Supporters: 0871 702 1972^
Email: Broxi@rangers.co.uk
Visit: www.rangers.co.uk

Headline News – Page 32

1. At Fir Park against Motherwell, Allan McGregor's stunning penalty save late in the game (after Madjid Bougherra had been dismissed) keeps Rangers unbeaten record intact.

2. In the Champions League, Madjid Bougherra scores a stunning equaliser against Stuttgart in the Mercedes-Benz Arena.

3. Rangers crush Motherwell 6-1 following goals from Miller (2), Lafferty (2), Boyd and Beasley.

4. With five goals in the 7-1 demolition of Dundee United, Kris Boyd's league tally of 160 confirms his position at the top of the all-time SPL scoring chart.

5. Allan McGregor's astonishing save from Samaras late in the Old Firm clash at Celtic Park keeps the score at 1-1.

6. With Hearts leading 1-0, Andrew Little's goal in stoppage time rescues a point.

7. Mo Edu fires the winner against Celtic at Ibrox in February.

8. Kenny Miller's stunning header wins the Co-operative Insurance Cup final for nine-man Rangers.

9. Back-to-back SPL championships are secured following Kyle Lafferty's goal against Hibernian at Easter Road.

Season 2009/10 Quiz – Page 33

1. Lee McCulloch

2. None – they were all 0-0 draws

3. Sasa Papac

4. Lee McCulloch (January) and Kenny Miller (May)

5. Motherwell and Dundee United respectively

6. 11

7. David Weir

8. 10 points

9. Andrew Little

10. 53 times – a world record

Who Said That Last Season? – Page 42

1. Kenny Miller (who scored a double in the opening 2008/09 Old Firm game) after his two goals against Celtic in October.

2. Walter Smith speaking about Sasa Papac.

3. Andrew Little speaking about his dramatic late equaliser against Hearts at Ibrox in January.

4. Former manager Alex McLeish talking about Nacho Novo.

5. Kenny Miller and his goal for nine-man Rangers in the Co-operative Insurance Cup final against St Mirren.

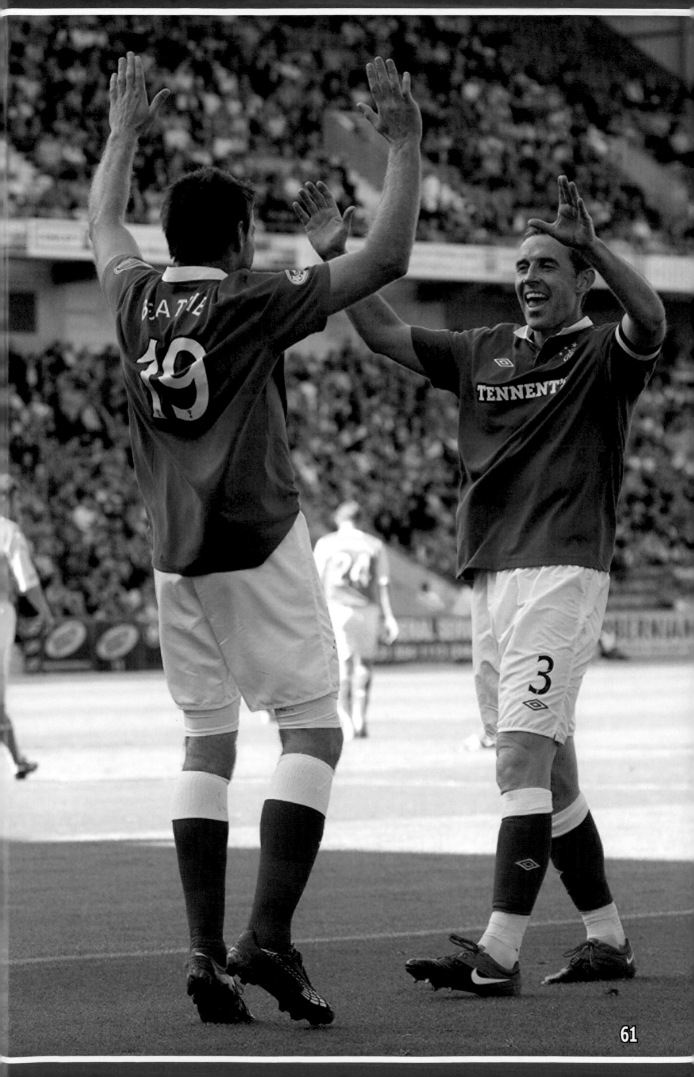

WHERE'S BROXI?

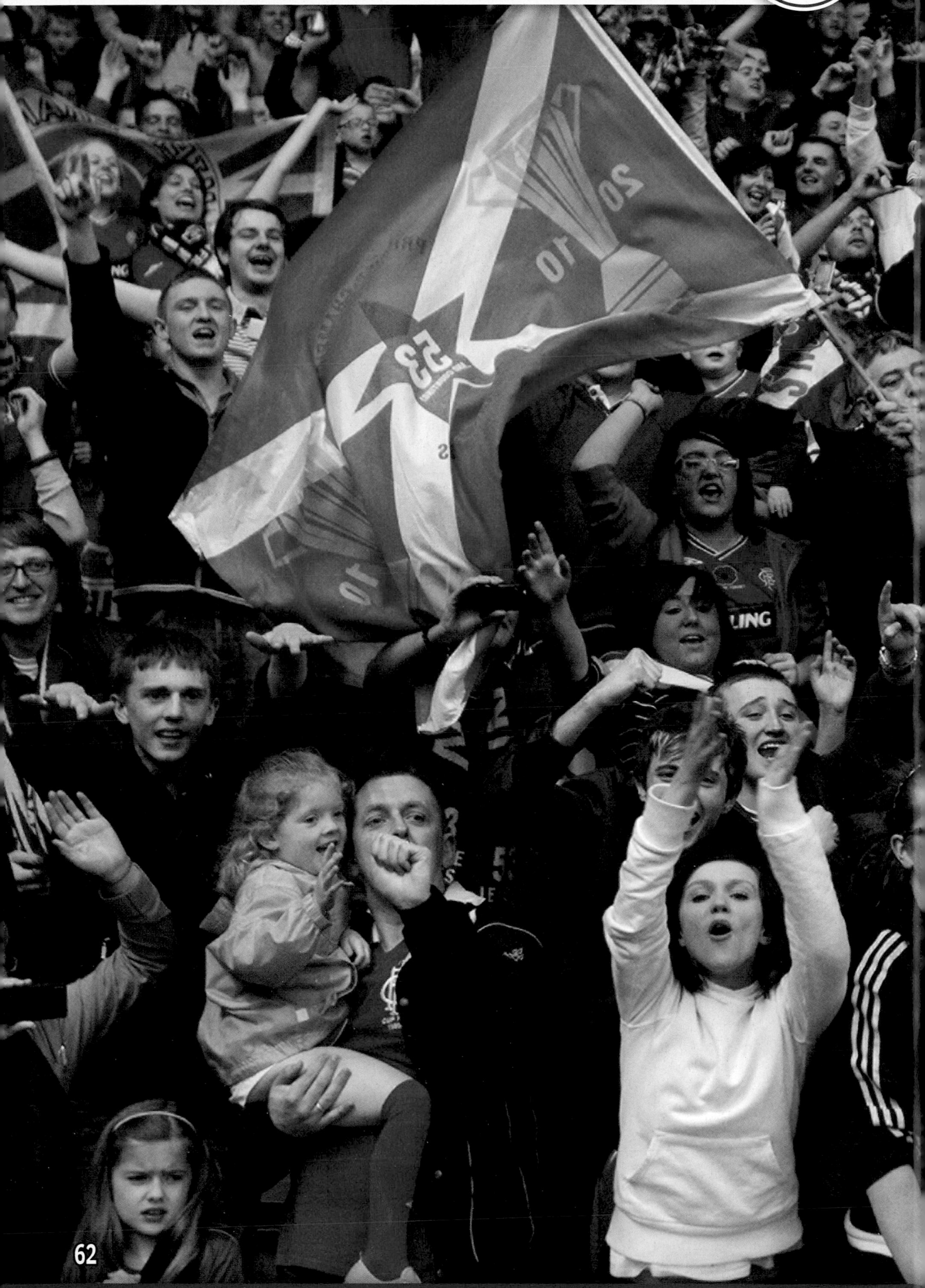

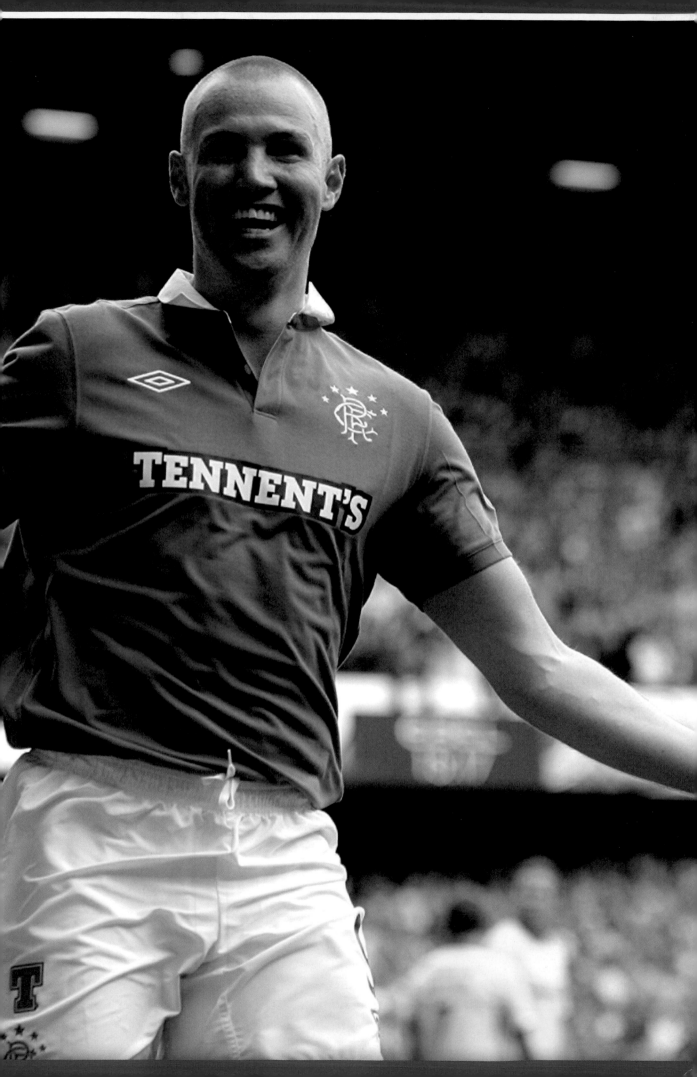